E-mail Etiquette
Made Easy!

Judith Kallos

Senatobia, MS, USA

ISBN: 978-1-4303-1381-6

Printed in the United States of America.

"To teach a man how he may learn to grow independently, and for himself, is perhaps the greatest service that one man can do another."
~ Benjamin Jowett

Acknowledgements

To my husband Paul and my
sister Jill for their ongoing support and
patience (SMTM). And, to the United States of America
for providing the opportunity to live the dream.

Contents

1

HELLO E-MAIL!

Who would have thought just a mere decade ago that e-mail would be so prevalent and to some the preferred mode of communication? I knew from the very beginning when I started my consulting practice TheIStudio.com over a decade ago that technology would change our lives.

But, if you think about it, none of us really have had any formal education or exposure to this new technology to fully understand the nuances and best practices of using technology properly with knowledge, understanding and courtesy. This easy guide will give you everything you need to know to use technology to its full benefit while ensuring that you don't appear to be a fish out of water.

You'll quickly see it is easy to practice proper E-mail Etiquette. As a matter of fact much of the information in this book you will discover is common sense while at the same time providing the answers to the questions you have probably wondered about.

At the same time you will learn how to be a joy to communicate with via e-mail, rather than having those you e-mail cringe when they see your name in their inbox.

All it will take is a little extra effort on your part to be perceived positively and to be able to take advantage of this new digital age both for personal enjoyment and professional gain. Remember my tag-line:

**"Using Technology with Knowledge,
Understanding and Courtesy." ™**

Remember, you can also find me online at NetManners.com and on my Blog which I post to several times each week, NetManners-Blog.com.

Are you ready? Let's get to work!

1

2

WHO NEEDS E-MAIL ETIQUETTTE?

Everyone who is online should want to use technology with knowledge, understanding and courtesy. The knowledge to use technology properly. The understanding about how your actions or lack there of can and will affect others. And, the courtesy that we as human beings should willingly want to show each other regardless of venue.

This is not an issue that only applies to certain people, countries or locations online. E-mail Etiquette applies to every one of us who chooses to participate.

It's hard to talk about E-mail Etiquette without running into the term Netiquette. What exactly is Netiquette?

Netiquette = <u>Network Etiquette</u>
E-mail Etiquette and Proper Technology Use

Netiquette has been around for decades before most even knew e-mail existed. Netiquette started as a simple group of guidelines to ensure that all who were using technology at that time were on the same page. Participants then knew what was expected of them as well as what they should expect from others.

Now that you know what Netiquette is, how is your e-mail etiquette?

- Do you forward e-mails to "all your friends" without thought as to which friends would really benefit or be interested in your forward?

- Or, do you e-mail Web sites asking for information they do in fact have online for your convenience simply because you don't want to take the time to read?

- Do you type in caps or all small case or fail to use proper sentence structure and grammar?

- Do you send unannounced large attachments that shut down the other side's e-mail box?

- Do you forward e-mails with everyone's e-mail address in the To: field?

These are **just a few** of the things that almost everyone has done at one time or another. Before they knew any better that is.

Common courtesy, social graces and socially acceptable behavior are terms used in a civilized society where humans interact with one another. Cyberspace is not any different. How you will be perceived, the type of human being that you are, your credibility and your level of education, integrity and ethics will be judged by how you choose to communicate with others online.

To minimize the importance of established guidelines (Remember, Netiquette has been around for decades!) is to make a conscious decision to be thought of as rude, lazy or possibly even uneducated. If you are online for commercial gain, lack of proper E-mail Etiquette could very well deter those who otherwise may have considered doing business with you. And wouldn't that be a shame?

Contrary to what some believe, the online world is not a free-for-all nor is E-mail Etiquette one person's opinion. And contrary to what some Bloggers or those who feel these issues are unimportant, I am not a techie sitting on the other side of a computer screen creating rules to annoy you or to infringe on your right to be inconsiderate if you so choose.

By the way, I am the furthest thing from your typical techie stereotype. I am passionate about the subject of E-mail Etiquette because these are the issues you need to know about and skills you need to hone to be considered someone people will enjoy communicating with.

4

I'll take you through the basic basics of E-mail Etiquette and much more in this book. No list of rules, no stuffy techo-babble. Just one onliner to another with hopes that you'll be so surprised at how much you'll learn and how easy it will be to apply!

3

THE BASIC BASICS

Let's cover the basic basics that you will want to minimally become familiar with in order to give a good impression.

Not typing in all caps or all small case.

Typing in all caps is considered yelling or screaming online. Even if you type only select words in your e-mail in all caps, it will be perceived as raising your voice – minimally adding emphasis.

Typing in all small case not only makes it look like you might not have made it out of grade school, and just as with all caps, your e-mails are more difficult to read. The eye relies on caps at the beginning of sentences to know when an idea or thought ends and a new one begins.

Proper case, sentence structure and grammar are simply necessary for clarity in your communications. Make the extra effort to use the shift key and you'll find you'll avoid misunderstandings and ongoing corrections from seasoned onliners.

Certainly if you are vision impaired and need to type in all caps a small comment to that affect to those you are communicating with will let them know you are not screaming at them. And, if you like typing with a larger font, which is your choice to make, do not make the assumption that others feel the same way. If you increase the font to create your e-mails, have the courtesy to return the font size back to its default size before clicking Send.

Do not leave the Subject: field blank.

Always fill in the Subject: field with a brief and concise description of the content of your e-mail. This is very important in helping those you communicate with organize and manage their e-mail activities and will be greatly appreciated by the other side. Here again, try to avoid using all caps or all small case, terms such as Hi, Help or Please Respond in the Subject: field as you may be misidentified as a spammer and your e-mail flagged as a spam and deleted.

Refrain from formatting your e-mails.

Did you know that fancy fonts, colored text and background colors or images most likely are not viewed as you intended by those you send to? You can't count on the other side having that font on their system or even have formatting turned on in the first place. Why risk your e-mail not displaying as you desire? Just type in plain text!

Use the BCc: Field

On those rare occasions where it is necessary to send a group of people the very same e-mail, as a courtesy to those you are sending to, please list all of the recipients e-mail addresses in the BCc: field. (Blind Carbon Copy - from the old days when typewriters used carbon paper to create identical copies of a document when it was being typed.) When an e-mail address is designated in the Blind Carbon Copy field, the recipient will get a copy of the e-mail while their e-mail address remains invisible and protected from the view of the other recipients of the same e-mail - some of whom they may not know.

You never want to expose your contact's e-mail addresses to strangers. If you are not sure how to BCc: in your e-mail program, here are several site resources that may help you learn the features of your software programs:

EUDORA: http://www.eudora.com/techsupport.
OUTLOOK EXPRESS:

http://support.microsoft.com/directory/faqs.asp?sd=gn&fr=0
SAFARI for Macs:
http://www.apple.com/macosx/features/safari/

Long lists of e-mail addresses at the beginning of any e-mail is an immediate sign that the sender is either a novice/Newbie - or doesn't care to respect other's privacy. None of which, as I am sure you'll agree, are complimentary perceptions!   E-mail addresses are like phone numbers. Only the owner of the e-mail address or phone number is the one to authorize who they want to have it and make it public to. Many folks prefer to decide for themselves who has their e-mail address.

By sending mass mails to a list of folks, you have made that decision for them - and that is a breach of assumed privacy when communicating with you. Let those you correspond with determine for themselves who they will make their e-mail address known to - do not make that decision for them! By listing handfuls of e-mail addresses in the e-mail headers for all to see is inconsiderate of each recipient's right to privacy.

Don't Forward "To All Your Friends"

If an e-mail states "forward to everyone you know" or something similar, that is a red flag to not do so. Read them if you must then hit Delete. Don't be tempted to forward those jokes, untruthful or frivolous e-mail that instructs you to forward to your friends!

You really don't believe e-mail that states certain things will happen simply by you forwarding the e-mail to 10 friends do you? No matter how noble the subject or even if it gives you a warm fuzzy, be selective and use your discretion on what you choose to forward to others.

In addition, many of these e-mails are actually hoaxes or downright bogus. Before you forward an e-mail that appears good intentioned with an incredible story that instructs you to "read and share" with everyone you know, first check Snopes.com to see if the story is even legit in the first place and not a hoax.

Not doing so can have you eating crow when everyone you e-mail is informed you just forwarded a hoax and didn't know any better.

Don't get mad if another onliner points out to you that you were uninformed by perpetuating a hoax. Avoid that embarrassment by doing your due diligence first. If you don't know for a fact that the e-mail you are forwarding is accurate and specifically apropos to the person you are forwarding to and you know they will want to receive it – don't forward at all.

One of the common requests I receive through NetManners.com is from folks wanting to know a "nice way" of telling someone they care about to stop sending joke, hoax and chain e-mails without hurting their feelings. Try not to put those you communicate with in this difficult position because you are only thinking of what you want to do at that moment. When it comes to e-mail it isn't all about you – there are those you are sending to who also should be considered.

Sharing of Personal Information

Never give out phone numbers, e-mail addresses or personal information without confirming you are communicating with a reputable party. Never give out personal contact information of others without their specific permission to do so.

Take the Time & Make the Effort

Make a reasonable effort to search a Web site for the information you are looking for - "Frequently Asked Questions" or "About Us" sections may give you the answers you seek before you waste the site owner's time by e-mailing for information that is readily available on their site. I get e-mailed daily for answers that are easily found in my Netiquette 101 or in the Internet 101 section if someone were to make minimal effort. These onliners simply didn't want to take the time to read them so they expected me to take the time to repeat what is on my site. Talk about giving the perception of lazy and not respecting other's time!

If a Web site owner takes the time to provide information; read it. If you do not find what you are looking for, search for the appropriate contact area for your question. Don't just click on the first e-mail link you come across and blurt out your question(s).

If you do, don't be surprised if your e-mail goes unanswered when the information is easily found on the site. It is important to understand the focus of each Web site as well. Each site cannot be everything to everyone or be what you perceive it should be. Be sure to review the information provided to double check that what you seek would even be covered by the site you are visiting.

Return Receipt & Priority Settings

You do not want to use the Return Receipt Request (RR) for each and every e-mail you send because you like "knowing" when someone opens your e-mail. Not only is this annoying to the recipient, this feature is intrusive! Would you like it if every time you heard a voice mail, answering machine message, opened a postal letter from a friend it was immediately reported back to them that you had heard/opened their communications? The recipient should have the privacy to determine when/if they want to open, read and reply - period.

RRs should be reserved for those instances where it is critical to each side knowing the e-mail was opened. Such instances would include legal and important business issues. However, keep in mind "opened" doesn't mean read and that the recipient can decline an RR request so you will not be notified of their actions.

The same applies to your e-mail and the Priority setting which specifies the priority of the message as it appears in the mailbox window. Setting every e-mail to the highest Priority is unnecessary and can cause this setting to be ignored.

Remember the boy who cried wolf?

Be Open to Learning and New Concepts

Understand that you will be on a continual learning curve. All of us are. This gig is changing constantly. The only consistency is change! If you do not have the desire to learn and do not make the effort to understand the "culture" of the technology in which you are participating, you will not be taken seriously by your fellow Netizens. You also may get some terse e-mails from other onliners pointing such issues out to you - some may not be as nice as others. When this happens, please don't fire back at them! Use situations like this as an opportunity to learn what you are doing wrong so you do not anger others and can have a more enjoyable time online.

Handling Nasty E-mails

If you receive a nasty e-mail - do not respond immediately - if at all. People are very bold and overly critical on the other side of their monitors. In my experience those who do not hesitate to point out the things they think you need improvement on do not notice the good or positive points on the very same issue. Many times these onliners are simply trying to get a rise out of you (this is called trolling) or are trying to make themselves feel self-important. Sometimes they are just plain jerks. If you do not have something nice or constructive to say, or at the very least sternly professional - just hit Delete.

E-mail and Copyright

Keep in mind that all private e-mail is considered to be copyrighted by the original author. If you post private e-mail to a public list or board, or forward it to an outside party in whole or in part, you must include the author's permission to post the material publicly. Not doing so can get you into some deep doo-doo legally or with your friends and associates.

Think of it this way... How would you feel if a personal private e-mail that you had written for a specific purpose/person is then plastered across the Internet or forwarded to those you do not know? Always ask for permission before forwarding or posting any private e-mails!

Managing Larger Attachments

Always minimize, compress or "zip" large files before sending. Many folks new to the online world do not realize how large documents, graphics or photo files are. Guess what? They are large enough to fill someone's e-mail box and cause their other mail to bounce! Get in the habit of compressing anything over 300,000 bytes (300K). (You can view file sizes in Windows Explorer. Simply right click on the file name and choose properties.)

There are several types of file compression software available for these purposes. Do a search at your favorite search engines for "file compression software" to view your options. You also want to refrain from sending unannounced large attachments to others because you think that photo or file is cute, cool or neat. Always ask first when would be the best time to send your attachments. More importantly when sending business files, do so only during business hours, always compress and send at a prearranged time.

Those online not too far outside of metropolitan areas do not have cable or DSL connections, they are on dial-ups! If you do not know how to compress files, then you need to learn how to make them physically smaller with graphic software. Those are your two choices; compressing or minimizing.

Minimizing a photo or graphic's physical size to no larger than 600 pixels in width will make them e-mailable. Most photos right off your digital camera are 1,000s of pixels in width which makes for a very, very, very large file size. Or you could be really courteous and learn how to use the free Web space offered by your ISP to upload photos and simply send the link to friends and family to view. If you do not know how to do any of these things all you have to do is learn! [Great Resource: HTML Programming Cheat Sheets for $3.95 at my eStore @ LearnAndThrive.com]

To send large files that take a long time to download that may not respect the other person's time, reflect their sense of humor or point of view and may even max out their e-mail box is pretty inconsiderate and downright lazy.

Virus Warnings

No need to forward virus warnings. Virus warnings received from others are generally always hoaxes. Definitely ignore those forwarded e-mails instructing you to delete files on your computer – the files that you are instructed to remove could be critical files that your computer needs to operate.

Only warn friends if you know that your computer has a virus that you inadvertently may have passed on to them. Rely only on your virus software and your software provider's Web site for the real scoop on this matter.

If you get one of these wacky e-mails from a friend or associate, go to your virus software provider's site and search for the virus name in question to confirm if it is accurate information or if it is a hoax. When you find it to be a hoax, let the person who forwarded it to you know that they are perpetrating misinformation and unintentionally alarming others.

Read what your Virus Software provider has to say before you unnecessarily alarm others and in the process end up looking rather silly to say the least. There are many urban legends purely in existence to watch all the Newbies screw up their computer's configuration files or forward the fake e-mail to "everyone they know" while looking rather foolish in the process. You know what they say... There's a Newbie born every minute!

With the advancement of technology, it is possible to get a virus without even opening an e-mail. Some of these e-mails merely require you click on the subject of the e-mail in your e-mail program or for those that use Outlook Express have your program set to preview so that the e-mail opens automatically. HINT: Turn Previewing Off!

Some viruses propagate by taking advantage of bugs in Microsoft servers to plant itself on the server and then transfer itself to those who visit the Web site on that server using Internet Explorer (yes, IE is buggy too) as their browser. Being Microsoft products are most used; they are naturally the main target of trouble-makers. That's why I use Eudora for e-mail and FireFox as my browser!

What many viruses can do is actually use e-mail addressed farmed out of your address book or inbox to send the virus and propagate itself to all those listed with your name or that of someone else in your address book in the From: field. The latest viruses can send out the virus using any combination of e-mail addresses found on your system! Yikes!

One thing is clear, the need for a 24/7 real-time virus protection software is no longer a choice - it is your responsibility to remain virus free. In addition, you need to update your virus files regularly. Check for updates every time you log on so that your computer is protected from the latest releases or use the convenient automatic update feature of your virus software.

Basics for Virus Protection

Get an active program that is always "ON". This will catch any viruses as they are being downloaded so they can immediately be quarantined and cannot infect your system.

Update your virus patterns daily or every time you log on. These updates can be downloaded from the Web site of your virus software manufacturer. Most software has a scheduler to tell your computer to do this automatically - how convenient! You need to ensure your system is protected from the latest viruses which may have just been discovered since last you were online. New viruses are identified daily!

Never click on any attachment or an .exe file attached within an e-mail without making sure the attachment has been checked for viruses. Even if the e-mail appears to come from someone you know very well! The attachment may be virus generated and plucked your friend's e-mail address off another infected computer belonging to someone they communicated with.

Or your friend may unknowingly be infected and not aware of the virus on their system which has just spawned an e-mail that has their name on it and is addressed to you. The e-mail may look like it is from your friend just to get you to open it when in fact it is an e-mail generated by a virus.

As a courtesy to your fellow Netizens, try to learn what virus protection is all about. Ignorance is not bliss online.

E-MAIL SOFTWARE TIPS

Your e-mail software settings and how you choose to use the features and functionality of your software can make a huge difference in your communications and in making e-mailing with you a pleasure not a pain. Add to that all the spam filtering software programs users and their ISPs have in place and your settings could have your e-mails misidentified as spam and not get to the intened party(s).

The From: Field

The From: field is key to your e-mail being recognized by those you send to. Make sure that your name displays formally:

John A. Doe

Not: john doe, john a doe, j doe.

Having your name display properly helps to ensure your e-mail is recognized by those who know you. By having it capitalized properly, you look like you made it out of the sixth grade!

It is simple little eNuances such as this that can make or break how you are perceived.

Filters and Rules

Do a search in your e-mail program's Help section to find an overview on how to use filters. In Outlook filters are called Rules.

What filters and rules allow you to do is set criteria based on incoming e-mail addresses, topics, and certain words that instruct your e-mail program on how to handle e-mails that meet those specifics.

For example you can have all the e-mail coming in and going out to your Mom's e-mail address go directly to your Mom Folder.

You can have all those e-mail that talk about enlarging certain parts of your body right to Trash – on the download. You'll never have to deal with those again.

Using filters greatly helps to organize and stream line your e-mail activity and are a great tool to become familiar with.

5

CREATING E-MAILS

With every e-mail you have the opportunity to communicate with clarity. The onus is on you as the author to ensure that the intent and tone you wish to relay is what comes across to those you e-mail. And, with every e-mail you also run the risk of being misunderstood or giving a less than positive impression by not paying attention to detail.

Remember; in e-mail you loose the benefit of eye-contact, body language, a firm handshake or a smile. By taking the time to create e-mails that have these 5 Essential Elements firmly in place, you ensure your meaning is not detracted from while minimizing possible negative perceptions and misunderstandings.

Every e-mail you write should have these 5 Essential Elements covered:

The From Field: Your name needs to be displayed properly. John F. Doe. Not john f doe, or john doe, j. doe or no name at all and only your e-mail address. Proper capitalization is very important here. When your name is in all small case you open the door to being perceived a spammer or worse yet - lacking education or tech savvy.

The Subject Line: A short, sweet and well thought out Subject is crucial and in some cases can help to ensure your e-mail gets opened. Keeping your Subject to 5-7 words that accurately identify the topic and context of your e-mail is imperative. Feel free to modify the Subject field in ongoing conversations to reflect when the direction or topic of the conversation has changed.

The Greeting: Without a greeting at the beginning of your e-mail you risk being viewed as bossy or terse. Take the time to include a Hello, or Hi and the recipient's name. How you type your contact's name (John, Mr. Doe, etc.) is indicative of the level of formality your e-mail will portray. Be careful to not take the liberty of being overly informal too quickly. Let the other side dictate the level of formality and follow their lead. After all, formality is just another form of courtesy. You can usually get an indication of how those you communicate with prefer to be addressed by how they sign-off their e-mails.

The Body: Taking the time to communicate with clarity is time well spent. Complete, correctly structured and capitalized sentences that reflect proper grammar and punctuation are crucial to your message. Typing in all small case or all caps does not lend to easy communications and gives the impression you are either lazy or illiterate. Review and spell-check every message before clicking Send.

The Closing: Whether it is "Thank you for your time!", "Sincerely", "Look forward to hearing from you!" or "Warm regards," use what is consistent with the tone and objective of your message. By not having a proper closing you increase the possibility that your e-mail will be perceived as demanding or curt. Without exception close by including your name to put that final considerate touch to your e-mails.

Make the effort to integrate these 5 Essential Elements in every e-mail you send and you will contribute to the perception that you are tech savvy, courteous and a pleasure to communicate with. When it comes to e-mail its all about communicating with knowledge, understanding and courtesy!

6

ARE YOU VIEWED AS RUDE?

All too often otherwise nice folks come off as terse or plain old rude when it comes to their e-mail habits. They don't intentionally set out to be viewed as rude, well I guess some do, but for the most part I prefer to believe the majority do not.

Are you being viewed as rude? Do your e-mail habits smack of a lack of consideration for the person on other side? Below are the most common faux pas I see onliners make on a regular basis that end up leaving a negative perception. If you answer yes to any of the following questions you are most likely being viewed as rude.

Do you forward e-mails without comment? If you cannot take the time to write a comment about why you are forwarding that particular e-mail to that particular person don't bother forwarding at all or you'll probably be viewed as rude!

Do you disregard requests from others who ask that you not forward e-mails to them? Not everyone wants to receive all those "informative" e-mails you feel are so important. Especially if you are forwarding without comment or thought by just clicking Send to your entire address book! Just because you can; doesn't mean you do! Honor their request to not forward e-mails to them with kindness and understanding. Otherwise, you will be viewed as rude (and selfish)!

Do you send overly large unexpected attachments? If you cannot take the time to determine file size and ask first when would be the best time to send them, you're being viewed as rude!

Do you send business attachments after business hours?
If you do, you will definitely be viewed as rude when you cause your associate's inbox to fill and all subsequent e-mail to bounce!

Do you start every e-mail with a "Hi" or "Hello" with the recipient's name and close with a "Sincerely," "Take Care," or TTYS and your name? If you cannot take the time to personally address an e-mail and sign off with courtesy, which will cause you to be perceived as demanding or curt, you'll be viewed as rude!

Do you e-mail Web sites for information without searching to see if the information you're seeking has already been provided for your convenience? If you cannot take a few moments to search a site and read the information provided, you'll be viewed as rude!

Do you use multiple !!! or ??? in your e-mails? If you do, you will come off as pushy and/or condescending and you will be viewed as rude!

Do you include everyone's e-mail address in the To: field even if they don't know each other? If you do, when you expose your contact's e-mail addresses to strangers that is a breach of privacy and you will be viewed as rude!

Do you add the e-mail address of new contacts, newsletters you've subscribed to or Web sites you receive e-mail from to your approved or white list? If not, your spam filters or your ISPs filtering program will return e-mails or ask for confirmation. If you initiated the request, add their e-mail address to make communicating with you easy or you'll be viewed as rude!

Avoid being viewed as rude by taking the time to have courtesy for the people you are communicating with. All too often folks think only of themselves and what they want to do at any given moment regardless of how it will be perceived or affect the person on the other side. Good manners never go out of style and that applies to your e-mail activities as well.

7

AVOID LOOKING SPAMMY

We all hate spam and get way too much of it! Now that we have that out of the way it is important to realize that in our zest to minimize our spam, we are deleting legitimate e-mails. Two factors are at play - not reviewing your trash before you empty it and on the other hand, sending e-mail with indicators that trip spam filters.

You need to make certain efforts so that your e-mail will not be inadvertently incorrectly perceived as spam. Several times each day, legitimate e-mail make it into my junk/trash due to the sender doing or not doing certain things that trigger most spam filters. These are issues you need to be aware of so that your e-mail has its best chance to make it to its intended party.

Here is a list of simple things to consider so that your e-mails are not mistakenly viewed as spam and deleted before read:

Always include an <u>appropriate, short and accurate</u> SUBJECT:. Many times spam does not have a SUBJECT: or it is malformed without appropriate text. Many e-mail programs auto delete subjectless e-mail to Junk/Trash. You also want to avoid using the words: stuff, hello, hi, help, new or the recipient's name or e-mail address as these will trigger spam filters.

Refrain from using common terms abused by spammers in your subject and/or first paragraph of your e-mail. You know what they are - you see them every day. Many spam filters track these terms and may inadvertently send your e-mail right to Trash.

Type your subject with appropriate capitalization and structure. All small case or all caps gives the impression of being spam (and lack of business technology skills).

Make sure your name is formally displayed in the FROM: field. Example: Jane A. Doe is correct. All lower case or lack of punctuation here indicates the lack of online savvy most spammers have and that your e-mail could be spam.

Refrain from using any formatting just for the sake of doing so. Formatting will trigger spam filters if not done properly.

When using any sort of spam software or filtering system, before you purge your trash, it doesn't hurt to take a quick peak to see if any e-mail is in fact from folks you know or recognize.

By keeping the above issues in mind, you have the best chance of your e-mail getting to the person on the other side.

REPLYING TO E-MAILS

Besides down-editing your e-mail which I will cover in a later chapter, there are only three considerations that you specifically need to be aware of when replying to e-mails from those who you know and communicate with:

Reply in a timely and concise manner. If you do not take the time to reply to the sender in a timely basis, they will think you are ignoring them. Yes, you may be busy, or your connection or computer may be causing you to be off-line, however, the other side will always assume your lack of response indicates you do not feel their correspondence is important to you.

If you are very busy and do not have the time to reply as you would like, pop off a quick e-mail stating you received the message and will respond in more detail as soon as you can. Then, follow through.

Certainly you do not need to reply to every e-mail that lands in your inbox. But for those that you have a relationship with, being courteous about your status and keeping them informed is simply the right thing to do.

Choose your words and how you use them carefully to ensure your intent and tone is accurate. There will be times that you receive an emotionally charged e-mail that screams for your response to set things straight. More times than not what you whip off on the keyboard at that moment in time would not be what you would send if you waited until the next morning to let cooler heads prevail.

The other side does not have your tone of voice, body language or eye contact to help them determine your intent. It is your job to make sure your meaning and tone are very clear and stated exactly the way you want them to be perceived. "I didn't mean it that way!" doesn't apply to e-mail -- if you type it, you had better mean it.

Don't reply based on assumptions. Even if you are a clear communicator you will run into those who are not or who do not take the necessary time as recommended above to ensure they are not misunderstood. And, there are those that will type their opinions without giving a single thought as to whether they sound rude, demanding or insincere.

In these cases; take the high road. No need to lower yourself to the same form of lazy communication. Take the time to address their points one-by-one so your reply is clear.

If you are unsure of their intent – ask before assuming and you'll find you'll avoid many an unnecessary misunderstanding.

TIP: A great way to set the tone of any reply or follow up e-mail is to use the Subject: field as a guide. Are you looking for the proper way to address e-mails that may be hot issues or need further assistance (asking for help, needing a response, clarification)?

What I do is use the Subject: field to help set expectations and the tone for my e-mails. Before the established Subject: on ongoing conversations I use:

FOLLOW UP:
FYI:
QUESTION:
UPDATE:

You could also use:

PLEASE RESPOND:
RESPONSE REQUIRED:
COMMENTS PLEASE:

You get the idea... This lets the other side know basically why I am replying to that specific subject and what I am looking for. You may also find that those you communicate with will appreciate this little "hint" in the Subject: field too!

9

FORWARDING E-MAILS

Forwarding of e-mails is one of the topics I get contacted about the most. And, one which also causes hurt feelings and misunderstandings more than any other topic. Daily, e-mails flow in from onliners asking about a "nice way" of telling someone they care about, relative, friend or associate to not forward attachments, chain e-mails, political commentary or the jokes that are so prevalent online.

Netizens are afraid to ask others to stop and those who are asked to stop, no matter how nicely, get offended and feel as though their thoughtfulness is not appreciated. But let's think about this a moment. How thoughtful is it to click the forward arrow, then a bunch of e-mail addresses and hit Send? Well, your brain had to "think" about those steps but does that make the effort truly "thoughtful." I don't think so...

Here are the 5 Rules of Forwarding E-mails that those who are being truly thoughtful follow. If everyone followed them all the problems associated with forwarded e-mails could be avoided. Sticking to these guidelines will assist both those thinking they are thoughtful and those who don't want to appear otherwise:

1. **Don't forward anything without editing out all the forwarding >>>>,** other e-mail addresses, headers and commentary from all the other forwarders. Don't make folks look amongst all the gobbly-gook to see what it is you thought was worth forwarding. If you must forward, only forward the actual "guts" or content of the e-mail that you are of the opinion is valuable. Check out this neato free program to help you out: Email Stripper:
   http://www.papercut.biz/emailStripper.htm

2. **If you cannot take the time to write a personal comment** at the top of your forwarded e-mail to the person you are sending to - then you shouldn't forward it at all.

3. **Think carefully about if what you are forwarding will be of value** (accurate information -- check for hoaxes @ Snopes.com), appreciated (something the recipient needs) or humorous (do they have the same sense of humor as you do) to the person on the other side. Or do you just think it is worthy? If you cannot think of why the person you are forwarding to would like to receive the e-mail - then don't forward it.

4. **It should go without saying** (But I have to say it because folks do so anyway.) that forwarding of chain letters; regardless how noble the topic may seem, virus warnings or anything that says "forward to everyone you know" simply shouldn't be forwarded because in most cases it is plain old B.S. (again check before forwarding @ Snopes.com). E-mail is e-mail - there is no chain to break or continue - no cause or effect whether you do or not. Also, the fact is not all commentary will be appreciated by the other side if they have a different viewpoint than you do - be very careful here.

5. **If you must forward to more than one person,** put your e-mail address in the TO: field and all the others you are sending to in the BCC field to protect their e-mail address from being published to those they do not know. This is a serious privacy issue! Do not perpetuate a breech of privacy started by other forwarders who included their contact's addresses in the To: or Cc: field by continuing to forward those visible addresses to your contacts! Remove any e-mail addresses in the body of the e-mail that have been forwarded by those who brush off the privacy of their friends and associates.

The above 5 rules will help qualify if an e-mail is worth forwarding and the right way to do so if it is. If one cannot make these extra efforts, then they really have no excuse to get mad or have hurt feelings when asked to stop. And if asked to stop forwarding, don't get mad; just realize the person on the other side certainly has the right to make that request.

On an aside, also keep in mind that if you are forwarding a private e-mail that was sent to you, you must get the sender's permission to forward it on to others (or post it publicly). E-mails are copyright protected by their authors. Not only that, common courtesy dictates that you should ask the author first if the e-mail sent for your eyes only can be forwarded to strangers or others for which it was not originally intended.

At the end of the day, when it comes to receiving unwanted forwarded e-mails, if you fear hurting someone's feelings by asking them to stop forwarding you e-mail, know they probably meant well, were really thinking of you, were trying to make a point - ahhh, just hit delete!

Irresponsible Forwarders Exposed!

Do you know an irresponsible forwarder or two, or three or five? Every so often they receive a nifty e-mail that cracks them up, has valuable information or worse yet is a hoax or contains controversial commentary that they then are possessed with the need to "forward to all your friends."

That's fine if done properly. However, as of late there is an increasing number of irresponsible forwarders who in forwarding to all they know make the heinous error of having all their friend's e-mail addresses visibility displayed in the To: or Cc: field. Without thinking, they have just exposed all their friend's addresses to total strangers!

What the majority fail to realize is that the only thing that list of contacts has in common is the Sender; otherwise all those listed are many times perfect strangers. Then to rub salt into the wound, these irresponsible forwarders perpetrate the breech of privacy created by the irresponsible forwarders before them by not removing the e-mail address of onliners they don't know from the body of the e-mail.

As if breeching their contact's privacy isn't bad enough these irresponsible forwarders are not thinking twice about perpetrating bogus information. They do not take the time to verify these forwards before they begin to forward something simply because the e-mail says to do so. It is every onliner's responsibility to make sure the e-mails they forward are not hoaxes so that they don't perpetuate passing on misinformation.

All one has to do is simply go to Snopes.com and search for the e-mail in question to confirm it isn't an urban legend or hoax before you hit that forward button. You are personally responsible for each e-mail you send just as you will be responsible when it is discovered you are forwarding erroneous information as if it were true.

Before you forward any previously forwarded e-mail, you need to take the time to remove any e-mail addresses of those you don't know before you forward the message along. Just because the person who forwarded to you was indiscreet and did not respect other's privacy does not mean you behave in the same manner. If you cannot take a moment to remove the visible e-mail addresses in the body of a message before forwarding it on, then you should not forward at all.

As if this perpetual breech of privacy is not enough to warrant a good spanking for all involved, what then happens is those onliners who have nothing in common but the Sender are then under the assumption that they can hit Reply to All: and send their opinions to everyone on the list. Many incorrectly presuming that it is O.K. to do so because those addresses are right there for the replying.

What then ensues is the Forwarder, who made the initial breech of privacy by not using the Bcc: field to contain all their contact's addresses, actually has the nerve to get upset. They scold their friend who hit Reply to All: telling them they had "no right" to e-mail *their* friends. Too funny! The Sender exposes their friend's e-mail addresses to people they don't know and then has the audacity to get irritated when those addresses are actually used. The initial fault lies with the Sender who could have easily avoided all of this by dutifully listing those e-mail addresses in the BCc: field.

When irresponsible forwarders behave in this manner, their friends are then open to receiving unwanted opinions from onliners they do not know. They understandably e-mail back with an attitude of "who the heck are you" providing the person who hit Reply to All: with a piece of their mind. Many times insults are hurled and name calling ensues. Other folks listed in the To: and Cc: fields join in; the flame war has now commenced!

There is an easy solution to this dilemma. Every time one feels the desire to "forward to all your friends" - respect their privacy by putting all e-mail address in the BCc: field or be prepared to face the music. And, if you have "friends" that expose your e-mail address in this manner to onliners you don't know; let them know in no uncertain terms that you don't appreciate their indiscretion.

Now you know how to be a responsible forwarder and respect other's privacy. Just a little extra thought and effort is all it takes.

10

E-MAIL AND PRIVACY

Do you show a blatant disregard for your contact's privacy? What if your contacts whether business or personal, decided to take your phone number and give it out to strangers? Strangers who you don't know! Strangers who may use your phone number to contact you about something you're not interested in or worse yet, who may sell your phone number to telemarketing companies to do the same.

The same thing happens with e-mail addresses every single day. We've all had this happen to us and it's not O.K. Each day we receive messages or forwarded e-mail from well intentioned onliners listing all those they are sending to in the To: field. And by doing so they are visibly displaying their contact's e-mail addresses to strangers!

If you do this and are thinking "no big deal" you are so wrong! If the only thing all the folks you are sending to have in common is you, you have breeched your contact's privacy by publicizing their e-mail addresses to people they don't know. Talk about showing a complete disregard for their privacy not to mention your lack of tech savvy!

Whenever you are sending to a group of onliners put your e-mail address in the To: field and everyone else's in the Bcc: field and protect their e-mail addresses from unnecessary exposure. Through my e-mail etiquette site, www.NetManners.com, I get inquires on a daily basis from folks who have been on the receiving end of such e-mail and there are two issues they ask me about:

1. How do I let this person know I don't appreciate them publicizing my e-mail address to people I don't know? What were they thinking!?

2. Is it O.K. to e-mail all the other people whose address is in the To: field along with mine about my business or service?

So as you can see, your contacts not only do not appreciate their e-mail addresses being made public without their permission but there are those that assume they can then spam those addresses because they are visible! By not respecting your contact's privacy you are in fact opening them up to additional unwanted e-mail.

Part of this problem is the BCc: is not in your face with some programs. In some cases it isn't easy to find and you have to search for the BCc: option. I use Eudora where the BCc: field is visible just waiting for you to put in e-mail addresses. However, for other software and Web based sites, here is what you do...

First, start a new message, then:

- In Outlook, if BCc: isn't showing, create a message, and from the View menu, click Bcc: Field.

- In Outlook Express, click View >All Headers.

- In Netscape, click the To: button then double-click BCc:.

- In AOL, put the BCc: addresses in the "Copy To" box, using parentheses and separating each address with a comma.

- In Yahoo!, click Add BCc:.

- BCc on Mac mail: Open a new email. In the bottom left of the title block is the Customize button. a menu opens, click on "BCc Address Field". This will appear on all future e-mails.

- Seamonkey: Click on the "To:" button and highlight "BCc".

The BCc: feature should be used when e-mailing a bunch of onliners who don't know each other because you don't want to publish other's e-mail addresses without their permission.

Show you "get it" and respect your contact's privacy! Wherever BCc: may hide, find it and use it!

Lastly, if you know a sender who doesn't respect their contact's privacy by using the Bcc: field, that does not give you permission to Reply to All: and send your most likely unwanted commentary to strangers. Be smarter than that and reply to the Sender alone. Let the Sender know your opinions about the subject matter of the forward as well as the fact that their apparent disregard for your privacy is not appreciated.

11

ONGOING E-MAIL CONVERSATIONS

Down-editing your e-mail is a necessary skill that adds to clarity in your communications and helps avoid misunderstandings. In addition, responding point by point to those who e-mail you also shows consideration for their time and your command of technology. It is a skill that is developed over time - by doing.

By editing your e-mail properly, you can leave that oh-so-important professional impression with those new business contacts who will be determining what it will be like to do business and communicate with you via e-mail. Since most onliners are anemic in this area - you will shine by making these simple efforts!

The first thing to remember is to never just hit Reply and start typing. Once you hit Reply, and type a courteous greeting, you should remove any part of the e-mail you are responding to that is not necessary to the clarity of the ongoing conversation. This includes e-mail headers (all that server and routing info at the top of some e-mail) and signature files. Here are some additional quick tips to help you on your way!

The best way to edit properly is to hold your left mouse button down and drag it over the text you want removed then hit delete.

Hit your enter key twice to put a line space between where you will type your response and the text you are replying to above. Then type your comments as it relates to the content above.

Continue to do the same as the e-mail continues. Remove what doesn't matter, leave what does, hit enter twice and type your reply.

What I do when I have removed a good bit of text is to type "<snip>" after a substantial deletion. This lets the other party know that I did in fact read that paragraph or portion of text but that either I have no comments specifically related to that area of the e-mail or that none are required.

E-mail becomes very difficult to follow when you start adding all the back and forth >>>>s. Make a habit of starting a new email after >>> are in the return. At that point most likely updating the SUBJECT: to better reflect the direction of the conversation will be in order as well. These efforts help avoid misunderstandings due to all the back and forth.

When replying to an ongoing series of e-mail where the SUBJECT: doesn't change, do what I do to keep your copies in order. Type "REPLY:" before the SUBJECT: field's content. Then as the back and forth continues type: REPLY [2], REPLY [3], REPLY [4], etc. This is a great way to have the order of the entire conversation visible at a glance while allowing your e-mail folders to keep the conversation in that order when sorted by SUBJECT:.

Integrating these steps when replying to e-mail can help keep your conversations on track and easier for all to read. Besides, by setting a proper example others can learn from you which is how most online learn new things. Now, in my book, that's as good a reason as any to get into the habit of down-editing your e-mails. Why not start today?

12

E-MAIL AUTORESPONDERS

E-mail autoresponders, also known as automatic replies or away/vacation messages are used quite often without a full understanding of how and when they should be used. While this e-mail tool has many effective and useful applications, there are also times when using an autoresponder is not recommended.

Here are five easy tips to help you use your autoresponders properly with knowledge, understanding and courtesy:

1. When using autoresponders for your business away message, engage the autoresponder just before your leave the office. Then, write yourself a note to disengage the autoresponder so it is one of the first things you do when upon your return. Nothing smacks of lack of organization or attention to detail than away messages still going out after you are back in the office and available for business communications.

2. A greeting and a closing including your name and title should be part of your away message. Business away messages should also include your name, the time-frame you will be unavailable as well as the name, phone number and e-mail address of someone that can be contacted in your absence.

3. Autoresponders used to confirm receipt of an inquiry or for disseminating commonly asked for information ("Click here to get our automated message on...") need to have an e-mail address in the From: field that is not the same as that of the autoresponder. Folks will hit reply to ask questions or give you their input. Rather than having them get another copy of what

they've already received, replies should go to a different account.

4. When subscribing to e-mail lists, forums, and discussion boards or when simply requesting information, refrain from using an e-mail address that has an automated response attached to it. Virtual loops can be created that can create literally thousands of back and forth e-mails when an address with an autoresponder makes a request to another e-mail address using an autoresponder. The inquirer makes their request, the request gets replied to by an autoresponder, the inquirer's autoresponder goes back to the address that responded which responds again and this back and forth will go on until one side or the other shuts down their autoresponders.

5. When engaging an autoresponder away message on an e-mail address that you know you have used to subscribe to e-mail lists, forums, Blogs or discussion boards, be sure to unsubscribe from all those services and resubscribe when you come back. This will prevent your message from being repeatedly sent out to those also subscribed who are not e-mailing you directly. To avoid this situation all together, have an e-mail address that you use specifically for such activities.

Autoresponders are a great tool and when used appropriately they can help keep others informed while freeing you up to do other things. Keep these issues in mind so that when you do use autoresponders, they are viewed as more of a benefit than an annoyance.

13

E-MAIL ATTACHMENTS

The topic of sending attachments by e-mail is not one that is discussed as much as it probably should be. It is easy to attach a file to an e-mail. Almost too easy! E-mail programs allow you to attach almost anything, regardless of the size and format without giving the sender any sort of guidance as to the consequences of their actions.

And yes, there are consequences. Like shutting down other's e-mail accounts and causing subsequent e-mail to bounce. Now, that's not a very nice thing to do, is it? And to think with just a bit of thoughtfulness you can avoid embarrassment and set an example of proper technology use!

Most that forward attachments or send photos along are doing so with good intentions not purposefully wanting to cause any problems for the other side. That said, though, one has to take a moment and think before attaching files to an e-mail and clicking Send. To simply attach files without taking the time to consider the person on the other side can come off as self-serving not to mention reflecting your overall lack of tech savvy.

Here are some quickies you should run through before you arbitrarily attach any file to an e-mail and send it on its way:

What is the file's size? If you don't know, find out. If you don't know how to find out, learn. For example in Windows, you can view the file's size in Windows Explorer. Make sure the Views option at the top right is set to Details. This will allow you to see a Size column reflecting each file's size.

If you are sending a file over 300,000 (300KB) in size consider how you can minimize the file's size either by reducing the physical dimensions or by using file compression software. And, even then, courtesy dictates you ask the recipient first if it is O.K. to send them an attachment and what is the best time of day to do so to ensure they are available to download your file and keep their e-mail flowing.

Never send attachments without warning especially after business hours or on weekends when the recipient may not be there to clear out their inbox.

Files over 1M (that's 1,000,000 bytes!) should not be sent by e-mail and will have a hard time going through the pipeline. Just because you can physically instruct a computer to attach a file of that size doesn't mean you should. You could also instruct your computer to reformat/erase your hard drive but you don't do you?

Files should only be sent in a format that you know the other side has the appropriate software to view - because you asked first! For example, not everyone has MS Publisher, Excel or PowerPoint. If the other side does not have Excel and you send an Excel file to them, they most likely will not be able to open it.

When it comes to graphics and photos, just assume the files are gargantuan. Whether the files are for business or personal matters, here again you need to compress either the file's size with one of the many compression utilities available or reduce the physical dimensions of the graphic or photo.

Learn how to resample/resize the graphic to no larger than 600 pixels in width. 600 pixels is large enough for the majority of uses - especially if you are just sharing photos with friends or family. For use on your Web site, they need not be larger than this either. Photos thousands of pixels wide easily get up into the 2-4M range! Yikes!!

Never send anyone an e-mail with an attachment about anything, (particularly your product or service) if the recipient did not specifically e-mail you for that information and you are responding to his or her request. By sending overly large files (even several personal photos) you can cause the other person's e-mail box to fill and all their subsequent e-mail to bounce.

You have no insight into the other person's e-mail volume to assume activity to be minimal or storage capacity to be optimal to receive your files. You do know what happens when you assume? Many e-mail accounts are only 5M in size and can be filled up very easily by those who either don't care to or don't know how to determine file size.

To send an attachment without notice that someone didn't ask for is the epitome of lack of courtesy for those you are e-mailing. No matter how important you think that attachment is - you now have no excuse to ignore the above issues when attaching it to an e-mail. Don't attach that file without first knowing its size, format and notifying the person on the other side that it is on its way.

Just a little common courtesy can go a long way to you being perceived as a person who is a pleasure to communicate with and who also understands the technology in which they are participating.

14

E-MAIL ORGANIZATION

Who doesn't have issues with organizing their inbox!? I receive close to 600 e-mails each day due to the variety of activities and contacts I have online. Some I am truly interested in their content - most I am not.

A big part of keeping your inbox and your e-mail organized is discipline. Yep, good ole' fashioned discipline! You need to make a consistent practice of checking your e-mail and accomplishing several tasks to keep ahead of the increased traffic of bits and bytes finding their way to your inbox.

What are we to do? Let's get organized!

1. Put your DELETE button to work! If you <u>do not recognize the sender,</u> look at the SUBJECT: field. Are there funny characters, alpha-numeric gibberish or it just doesn't make sense? Delete! Don't fall for tricky SUBJECT: fields that say any number of enticing comments only someone you know would say: "Get a $500 Cash Advance Overnight!", "They said it's free!", "Hey how is it going?", "RE: Account #", "Meeting is Rescheduled", or the one almost everyone wants to open "About Your Tax Refund".

    None of these are from friends or folks you know or even companies you are doing business with. They are from spammers - the worst kind too - the ones who underestimate your intelligence by thinking these e-mails will be something you would take seriously. If you don't know the sender and the SUBJECT: field looks off, send them on their way to the trash!

2. Once you go through all your new e-mail and follow step #1 above, you are now ready to determine what to do with the e-mails that are left. Do you have several e-mails from the same party? Do you have e-mail from folks who e-mail you quite regularly? Do you have some e-mail that is personal business and others that are more serious and therefore, you probably need to keep a copy on hand? This is where filters come in. Filters are your friends! Filters, or Rules as they are called in Outlook, are what allow you to organize your e-mail on the download. Yes, as you download your e-mail it can go into e-mail folders setup for specific topics or contacts!

You can have a "Mom" filter that sends all e-mail from dear old Mom right into your Mom folder. Set up filters to have e-mail from some of your hobby sites, go directly into their own folder. Your best friend can have his or her own folder. Another example is to have information from your financial institutions automatically end up in a folder specifically divided into further folders - Annuity, CDs, Stock, Bonds. The sky is the limit!

A side benefit of filters is that if you organize your e-mail to go into their own folders on download - your inbox has less e-mail that you requested or were expecting leaving only the questionable e-mail for you to review. Filters only need be setup once and they are in place until you delete them. Get your filters tightly setup and you can literally find only e-mail from spammers are left in your inbox.

One thing is clear about being online and e-mailing - it behooves you to become familiar and proficient with your tools. E-mail software being probably the most important. Check the HELP area or Web site of your e-mail software for further guidance on filters or rules. This is reading and skill building well worth the time when you realize how easily you can control your e-mail's organization moving forward.

Shameless Plug: Check out my Outlook heavy-duty laminated cheat sheets! These software guides give you the tips you want at your fingertips to accomplish the task at hand. At my eStore LearnAndThrive.com. (Apropos don't you think?)

3. Another use for your filters? As if filters are not already sounding like the best thing since sliced bread, you can use them to send certain e-mail right to the trash bypassing your inbox all together! You know, the e-mails for Viagra and adult sites - right to trash. Filters and rules can be used to not only send an e-mail to a certain folder by virtue of the e-mail address, company or person's name, they can be configured to find certain adult or offensive terms when listed in the SUBJECT: or BODY of an e-mail message so you can send them right to trash on the download - gotta love it!

4. Back to your inbox... We now have filters in place that organize your e-mail on the download so all the e-mail you requested and or are expecting, is in their appropriate folders for you to read at your convenience. Now your inbox should only have the orphan e-mail with nowhere to go. After following the suggestions above, begin to review your e-mail. If you run into an e-mail that is from a new mailing list you've subscribed to and plan on getting regular e-mail from, stop right there and make a folder and filter to accommodate these future e-mail. Set up a filter to look for something specific to that e-mail (usually the e-mail address works best) and moving forward, on the download, those e-mails will go right into their own folder. Do this for any e-mail topic or contact you plan to receive e-mail from on a regular basis.

5. Read and delete. Read your e-mail as time permits and then delete any e-mail that doesn't have content worth keeping for future reference. Then, empty your trash daily. Loads of e-mail files use a ton of your system's resources. Not keeping copies of e-mail you really will never need in the future helps remove the clutter and drain on system resources.

6. When reading your e-mail you can prioritize each message by color-coding it. Many e-mail programs allow you to label e-mail by color when viewing a particular folder. For example you could have labels that at a glance tell you how you have

prioritized your tasks. Say, red for urgent, blue for later, yellow for maybe. By opening that specific e-mail box you know, at a glance, which e-mail you have set to address right away and which you can get to as time permits.

7. Empty your trash daily but before emptying your trash, you want to be sure to take a quick look-see just in case any of your filters inadvertently picked up on some terms that were included in e-mail that you possibly didn't want to trash. This happens all the time! A quick once-over before deleting your trash will ensure legitimate e-mail you do want to see didn't get lost in the shuffle.

8. Create a folder called Follow-Up, Interesting or To Do. This is where you will file some of the e-mail from your inbox that peaked your interest that you would like to review in more detail but just don't have the time. Then, when time permits you can go to that folder and check into the e-mails worth keeping. Once you review them, though, either send them to another folder for keeps or send them to trash.

9. To avoid e-mail backup, be sure your inbox is cleared each day. Move e-mail to trash, a specific folder or your "To Do" folder, and then empty the trash. If e-mail is older than 90 days in your "To Do" folder - send them off to trash as most likely the information or offer is no longer current. By doing so each day, you keep your inbox clear and your e-mail much more organized.

10. What about all these folders? Have as many folders as you need to be organized and call them whatever will intuitively work for you with a glance. This system is different and unique to each and every user - make sure you use terms and a system that works for you.

The above 10 tips when practiced daily will make the world of difference in keeping your inbox organized and clutter free. Just a bit of discipline is all it takes to be on the road to less time spent dealing with e-mail which frees you up to do other important things....like responding to e-mail.

15

UNDELIVERABLE E-MAILS

There several common reasons you may receive undeliverable e-mail returns:

- You had a typo in the e-mail address making it incorrect and therefore undeliverable. Conducive to dialing an wrong phone number.

- The person you are e-mailing actually gave you an incorrect e-mail address (typo) - that happens allot!!

- Their inbox is filled to capacity due to large attachments or not logging in for a while. Another cause is they have "leave mail on server" checked in their e-mail program which then does not allow their e-mail account to be cleared as all e-mail is "left on the server". Until that option is unchecked and all e-mail is downloaded to clear out their e-mail account this will continue to happen. Leave this option unchecked unless you can micro-manage it!

- A spammer used a phony e-mail address when sending to you and your autoresponder message could not respond to the bogus e-mail address.

- Someone who has your e-mail address on their system has a virus that is propagating itself to old or non-existent e-mail addresses putting your address in the FROM: field. This causes undeliverable virus generated e-mails to be returned to you.

Undeliverable error messages are the protocol in place to let you know when messages sent do not (for many different reasons) make it to the intended recipient. You want to become familiar with how these messages relay exactly what the problem is.

With all returned e-mails, there will always be an "undeliverable reason" at the top of the e-mail as to why the message could not be delivered. If you look closely at the returned message you will see what the problem was. The top of the message will look similar to this:

The original message was received at Thu, 12 Jun 2003 18:45:05 - 0500 (EST) from tiberius-t.isp.net [207.69.232.22] ----- The following addresses had permanent fatal errors ----- ----- Transcript of session follows ----- ... while talking to mx.xxxxx.xx.com. >>> RCPT To: <<< 550 ... User unknown 550 ... User unknown

The above reflects that there is no such e-mail address on that system - user unknown. Here is a listing of the most common error codes you will see in undeliverable e-mails and what they mean:

- 251 User not local; will forward to 421 Service not available, closing transmission channel
- 450 Requested mail action not taken: mailbox unavailable (E.g., mailbox busy)
- 451 Requested action aborted: local error in processing
- 452 Requested action not taken: insufficient system storage
- 500 Syntax error, command unrecognized
- 501 Syntax error in parameters or arguments
- 502 Command not implemented
- 503 Bad sequence of commands
- 504 Command parameter not implemented
- 550 Requested action not taken: mailbox unavailable (E.g., mailbox not found, no access)
- 551 User not local
- 552 Requested mail action aborted: exceeded storage allocation (mailbox filled)

- 553 Requested action not taken: mailbox name not allowed (E.g., mailbox syntax incorrect)
- 554 Transaction failed

These messages vary depending on the systems involved in the delivery of the e-mail. And, you will always see the e-mail that could not be delivered below the error message to see if it is in fact an e-mail you sent, your autoresponder or a virus generated e-mail that you did not send.

16

E-MAIL WHITELIST ETIQUETTE

A big-time dilemma is brewing online. In an understandable attempt to bypass all that annoying spam, e-mails that onliners want to receive are getting lost in the shuffle. Newsletter subscription requests are not being completed and important e-mails are not getting to their intended parties. This is why I no longer send out my quarterly newsletter. For all the work that went into putting my newsletter together, the hassle of it not getting through made the effort no longer productive.

Your "Whitelist" is the list that contains the e-mail addresses of those you do in fact want to receive e-mail from. Some services require the accepted addresses be in one's address book to be added to the whitelist. While other software/services call this list the approved or allowed senders list and require you manually add those you want to accept e-mail from to your list. Regardless of what this feature is called, it is clearly not being utilized correctly and in many cases, at all.

What can be done about this? A little user education and E-mail Whitelist Etiquette is in order!

- When signing up for an online newsletter, mailing list or Web site service, immediately add their e-mail address or dot com to your approved or white list. This will ensure smooth communications with you and that e-mails will get through with the information you requested or confirmations necessary for you to acknowledge your request.

   o **AOL:** Place the domain name you just signed up for a service at in your address book.

○ **HotMail:** Place the domain name within your "safe list". You can locate your safe list by clicking on the "Options" link next to the Main Menu tabs.

○ **Yahoo!:** If the e-mail you requested ends up being filtered into your "bulk" folder, all you have to do is open the e-mail and click on the link next to the "From" field.

○ **Other ISPs and Providers:** To prevent desired e-mails from being sent to trash, try adding the e-mail's "From" and "Reply to" address to your address book.

• If you initiate the request, it is your responsibility to promptly add the other side's e-mail address or dot com information to your whitelist. This extra step will reflect that you are courteous and tech savvy! In addition, doing so will avoid those who you have requested information or services from, from having to follow verification e-mail instructions just to get you the information you requested. Besides, you cannot count on everyone responding to those verification e-mails-many simply don't or can't (automated subscription systems).

• Before getting upset because you perceive someone didn't respond, check to see if their e-mail was inadvertently deleted or sent to your Trash or Junk folder. Then, upon finding these e-mails in your Trash or Junk folders, add their information to your whitelist straight away. Too many onliners become belligerent about a supposed lack of response when in fact a response was sent and because they didn't clear the way for the e-mail to be accepted it was diverted to trash or not allowed through.

• Web sites and newsletters should have a response or thank you page that clearly requests site visitors and subscribers to add the required e-mail address to their whitelist right then and there. If onliners know the address to expect e-mail from, it is much easier to expect that they will add that address to their whitelist and your e-mail will get through.

It is important that every onliner make a conscious effort to become aware of the above issues and integrate these suggestions into their day-to-day activities. Only then can an informed online community use e-mail for the efficient and convenient communication tool it was meant to be.

17

HANDLING RUDE E-MAILS

As of late, online has been a bit "off". Not sure if it is the unusually strong solar flares, full moon or the fact Mars is closer to Earth that it has been or will be for 1,000s of years. Rude and crass e-mail seems to be at an all time high. E-mails blurting out demands or questions without the courtesy of a decent subject field or a thank you to follow. Questions or requests that are demanding a reply without the courtesy of a hello, or a closing that notes their name.

Could it be because manners seem to be at an all time low off-line? Combine this with folks not learning the power of the written word or the skills to communicate clearly to reflect their tone and intent and you have a volatile combination. There are two assumptions here. The first being that anything goes online. There are no rules, you can do what you want - period - and don't try to tell anyone differently.

Proof in point, I am spammed at least once each month through my site's contact form by someone typing in caps and/or profanities questioning my content and opinions at NetManners.com.

Who do I think I was even implying that folks be courteous? The Internet is a "free-for-all" and there are no rules!! Then, as those who e-mail in that manner usually do, their protest e-mails use a bogus e-mail address so I could not respond. So typical of those who react in that way to what they don't want to hear or make the effort to learn. They literally prove my point on this topic!

Secondly and a big contributor, is the belief that there is no good reason (even if there actually is one) for anyone to not say what they want when they want (freedom of speech) or have what they want, when they want it and how they want it. Consideration for other's feelings and opinions don't matter when you can tap out some uninformed crudeness and hit Send.

Folks are quite bold in the anonymity being behind this screen offers them. Some fly off the handle without reading an entire site, article, thread or e-mail, many times picking out parts to create a manifesto of opposition without actually looking at the big picture of the topic at hand.

Those who are uninformed with a lack of attention to detail do not hesitate to spew their self-important opinions that many times are not based in fact or reality. Misunderstandings occur, business is lost, and feelings get hurt. All because there are onliners who do not take the time to communicate carefully with the written word by integrating courtesy and clarity.

What do you do when you are the recipient of an e-mail with and accusatory or rude tone? Well, I used to be a firm believer that you should respond to every e-mail someone takes the time to send you - that is everything but spam. However, as of late, I have even found myself at a loss for words when reading some of the e-mail that has come my way. Site visitors who don't know me using verbiage that makes my cheeks flush!

Unfortunately, I think all of us will have to deal with these "personalities" at one time or another and probably more so that any of us prefer. Here are some thoughts to help you determine if and how to deal with rude or nasty e-mail:

- If you receive an e-mail with foul language or threats, know that this is against the TOS (Terms of Service) of all ISPs. Immediately send the e-mail to abuse@ at their ISP connectivity provider (not their business or personal domain address.). Keep the e-mail on file in case you need to refer to it or provide additional copies down the road.

- When you receive an e-mail that is blatantly rude or obnoxious and is not based in fact, think about if there is any constructive reason to have to respond. If the tone is so bad that you feel your blood pressure rise, wait until the next morning at the very least to even think about if you need to respond. Your ego is not large enough (I hope) to have the need to defend yourself when faced with incorrect accusations or personal digs, especially from onliners who don't know you. Don't lower yourself to their level by responding to this type of e-mail in kind. Hold yourself to a higher ground and do not respond at all, regardless of the tone or accusations within the e-mail in question.

- If someone e-mails you because they are misinformed, did not take the time to read the information on your site or a post somewhere online or possibly could have made an honest mistake, "kill" them with kindness and give them the benefit of the doubt. Most truly do not know how they are perceived by virtue of their lack of e-mail skills, nor do they expect you to take them at their word. All too often you'll hear "I didn't mean it that way...." Well, I have a saying around here, if you type it, you'd better mean it!

- Folks who e-mail in this manner simply do not realize the power of their words and the tone they are setting. Point out in a courteous manner the information to correct the issue or point them to the area on your site or elsewhere that has the info they seek without personalizing the issue. Thank them for contacting you, sign off in a professional manner and hold your head high knowing you just provided a level of courtesy that is quite rare online. You may even be surprised when that very same Netizen sends you a thank you e-mail! That being said, with some onliners there is nothing you can do to sway them. You can be correct, courteous and clear and it won't matter - they simply will not admit to being misinformed or plain old wrong. Don't take it personally, rather feel sorry for anyone with a mind that closed and move on.

Because you have a Web site, are visible in online forums, or are available via e-mail in no way means that you have the responsibility to respond to those who do not communicate with you in a respectful courteous manner. And, most likely those who do not communicate with courtesy and knowledge are folks none of us would care to form a relationship with or do business with anyway. So, don't let worrying about loosing that online "friend" or business "lead" have you lower your standards in regard to how you want to be treated.

I receive on average over 600 e-mails each day. Most are positive and many are simply wonderful written by great people across the globe that have been to one of my sites and are asking my assistance or advice. However, for those increasing number of onliners who think they can just e-mail and make accusations, rude statements, demands or requests without a hint of courtesy or consideration, well, they won't be hearing from me - DELETE!

18

ACRONYMS

Acronym: Abbreviations of commonly used phrases as used in e-mail. Acronyms are not an excuse to not spell out words or to type cryptically. There is a time and place for their use, and they should be used sparingly and only when appropriate (i.e., not in your resume). Below are some typical acronyms you will encounter in your online communications.

Once online for even a short time you will find an acronym for almost any situation. To get you started, here is a list of the most commonly acronyms used in e-mail, message boards, and IM.

ACRONYM	MEANING
AFAIK	\As Far As I Know
BBL	Be Back Later
BFN	Bye for Now
BRB	Be Right Back
BTW	By The Way
FUBAR	"Fixed" Up Beyond All Recognition
FB	Files Busy
FWIW	For What It's Worth
FYI	For Your Information
g	Grin (usually in brackets)
gd&h	grinning, ducking, and hiding
gd&r	grinning, ducking, and running
HSIK	How Should I Know
IAE	In Any Event
IANAL	I Am Not A Lawyer
IMO	In My Opinion

IMHO	In My Humble Opinion
IOW	In Other Words
JFYI	Just For Your Information
LOL	Laughing Out Loud
LMAO	Laughing My —— Off
NBD	No Big Deal
NOYB	None Of Your Business
OIC	Oh, I See
OTL	Out To Lunch
OTOH	On The Other Hand
PITA	Pain In The A——
PMFJI	Pardon Me For Jumping In
PTB	Powers That Be
RSN	Real Soon Now
RTFM	Read The "Fine" Manual
S	Smile (big S, small s)
TANJ	There Ain't No Justice
TIA	Thanks In Advance
TIC	Tongue In Cheek
TPTB	The Powers That Be
TTFN	Ta Ta For Now
TTYL	Talk To You Later
TYVM	Thank You Very Much
VBG	Very Big Grin
WOA	Work Of Art
WTH	What The H——
WYSIWYG	What You See Is What You Get

19

EMOTICONS

Emoticon: A figure created in e-mail using the symbols on the keyboard. Read with the head tilted to the left. Used to convey the spirit in which a line of text is typed. With e-mail you will communicate with people who may not know you; they cannot see your facial expressions or body language. This lends to the misunderstandings which I get contacted about for advice all the time. Also known as "smileys" these symbols will help others know where you are coming from and to make the intent of your typed comments clear. If you don't use Emoticons and your e-mail is misunderstood, it is your own fault.

Here for your convenience, I have listed some of the most common as well as those only for comic relief:

EMOTICON	MEANING
:-I	Semi-smiley
:-%	User has a beard
:-=)	Older user with mustache
:-\	Undecided user
:-p	User is sticking their tongue out
:-'|	User has a cold
:-)8	User is dressed up
:-D	User has a big mouth
:-#	User's lips are sealed.
:-o	User is shocked, surprised.
:-s	User after a *bizarre* comment.

:-{	User has a mustache
:-|	No-expression face
-:-)	User sports a Mohawk
:^$	Put your money where your mouth is
:-&	User which is tongue-tied
:-9	User licking its lips
:-(	Sad
:-X	User is wearing a bow tie
:-7	User after a wry statement
:-@	User is screaming
:-%	User is a banker
:-)	Humor (or smiley)
:-))	Big smile or grin
:-c	Bummed-out smiley
:-Q	Smoker
;-)	Winking smiley
(-:	User is left-handed
{(:-)	User is wearing toupee
+-(:-)	User is the pope
*:o)	User is a bozo
*<|:-)	User is Santa Claus (ho ho ho)
]:-}>	User is a "little devil"
=:-)	Smiley punk rocker
|-)	User is asleep (boredom)
8-)	User wears glasses
8:-)	Glasses on forehead
o-)	User is a Cyclops
{	User is Alfred Hitchcock
@-}---}---	A rose

20

GLOSSARY

Here is a collection of some of the terms you may run into during your online activities. In addition, some of the terminology listed will give you a brief history of the Internet and World Wide Web that you were not aware of.

ARPA: This stands for Advanced Research Projects Agency, an arm of the U.S. Department of Defense, and the agency that created the ARPAnet.

ARPAnet: A network started in the 1960s by the Advanced Research Projects Agency (ARPA) to connect several research institutions and laboratories. The goal was twofold: first, to coordinate research among similar labs; and second, to create a completely decentralized network. The Department of Defense wanted a network that could withstand a nuclear attack on the United States. Because the net is decentralized, there is no central computer to knock out. In recent years, this has been both a burden and a help. On one hand, no censorship can occur (except as unwritten rules enforced by the users themselves). But on the other hand, the Internet's growth has made it increasingly difficult to find anything. Unlike the local phone company, it is nearly impossible to find a complete "white pages," since there is no central governing body to catalog the net's features. (By the way, the ARPAnet was turned off in 1986. It was a miracle of decentralization that, when ARPAnet was shut down, no one but the system operators knew about it.)

ASCII: The American Standard Code for Information Interchange, a standard way of representing text. ASCII text contains no formatting. This makes it handy for sending among computers on multiple platforms e.g., between IBMs and Macs. ASCII is the standard language of Internet e-mail and newsgroup text, among other things.

Browser: A program used to view World Wide Web pages. Most Web browsers also can access WAIS, Gopher, FTP, and telnet. The browser reads the HTML and other programming codes to display the pages as you see them. Microsoft Internet Explorer, Mozilla, Opera, and Netscape are the most popular browsers.

Cache: The cache file in your browser remembers every Web site you have been to. This enables you to keep clicking on the browser's Back button to go to the pages you were at previously without waiting for them to have to download again. If you are not going to use the information in this file after you log off, it is a good idea to get in the habit of clearing out the cache at the end of every session. Many browsers also allow you to determine the cache size and when it should be cleared.

CERN: The European Center for Nuclear Research, the organization that created the World Wide Web in 1989. Remember this the next time you play trivial pursuit!

DNS: The Domain Name System, a standard way of stating Internet addresses. There are specific ending addresses called "top-level domains," such as "com" depending upon what the address refers to. Below are the most commonly used domain suffixes; however, now there is a suffix for almost every country on the planet Earth.

EXAMPLE DOMAIN SUFFIX	STANDS FOR:
.edu	Educational Institution
.org	Nonprofit Organization
.gov	Government

.com	Commercial
.biz	Business
.ws	World Site
.us	United States
.mil	Military Address
.ca	In Canada
.cn	In China
.fr	In France
.de	In Germany
.uk	In the United Kingdom

Emoticon ("Smiley"): Certain characters that some people use to help express emotion in e-mail. The most common is :-). With a little imagination and a tilt of your head, you may see that this is a smiley face. All of these faces are to help express different emotions with recent programs now available that offer little smiley graphics in lieu of their plain text counterparts. It is important when you e-mail, that you use emoticons to relay the tone of your e-mail. If you crack a joke and don't utilize a smiley, the other party may not know you are joking and may misinterpret your e-mail.

FAQ: Stands for **F**requently **A**sked **Q**uestions and is a common term used on the Internet. When visiting a Web site looking for information, the first place to check out is the Web site's FAQ. Most likely many of your questions, which have been asked by previous visitors, will be listed for your reference.

Flame/Flame War: A very harsh message from one person to another, mostly in newsgroups. Flames are often directed at newbies or those who are being troublemakers. The harshness in them is usually not intelligent commentary or a debate on a difference of opinion. Normally, it is just an insult hurled by a jerk who does not know how to communicate civilly and with clarity. Huge "flame wars" can often erupt around volatile issues. It is always best to avoid these situations as continuing the "conversation" is unlikely to change anyone's opinion. What we learned from our mothers applies here: "If you can't say something nice don't say anything at all."

Freeware: Free software. Also see shareware and public domain.

FTP: **F**ile **T**ransfer **P**rotocol. This is one standardized way of transmitting files on the Internet. As with most services on the Internet, there are specific FTP servers containing specific types of files. Due to the popularity of technology in the last decade, FTP has now become a verb. As an example, you will hear people say "FTP it to your computer."

Home Page: A space on the World Wide Web where companies and individuals have information post about themselves. Many people and businesses refer to their Web Sites as their Home Page. Increasingly, however, "home page" is now more likely to be used in the context of a personal noncommercial Web site.

HTML: **H**ypertext **M**arkup **L**anguage is the standard way in which all World Wide Web pages are written. It is read using browsers such as Opera, Mozilla, Netscape, and Microsoft Internet Explorer.

HTTP: **H**ypertext **T**ransfer **P**rotocol. Much like FTP, this is just another way of sending material across the global network. HTTP is specifically used to send World Wide Web pages across the Internet.

IRC: **I**nternet **R**elay **C**hat is a method of conducting live chats on the Internet. It is sort of like a CB radio, in that people can choose whichever channel they want and then chat with whoever is on that channel. This can mean thousands of people chatting at once. At times this is practically unmanageable and not very enjoyable. Many Web sites now offer chats where additional software or plug-ins is not necessary.

Link: Whenever text on a Web page is in a different color than the majority of text, and is underlined, or changes colors when your mouse pointer hovers over it, this is referred to as a link. Links can take you to another area at that Web site or to another site on the Web. When you click on a link, your browser will take you to the designated place the link calls out. You will notice that most links will change to a different color once you click on them. This is a visual to you to let you know you have "been there, done that."

Lurker or Lurking: A lurker is one who reads postings in forums or newsgroups without responding or participating. Before jumping into any discussion area, initially it is a good idea to be a lurker before posting to determine the rules and personality of the group. Don't want to unnecessarily step on any toes now, do we?

Mailing List: A subject discussion area that is much like a newsgroup. The main difference between a mailing list and a newsgroup is that a mailing list is performed by e-mail, while newsgroups are not. People send messages about topics to a central computer, and then the mailing list program distributes the message to everyone who has subscribed to the list.

MIME: Multipurpose Internet Mail Extensions is a protocol for attaching nontext files (e.g., graphics or programs) to e-mail messages. The only caveat to sending a MIME message is that the person receiving the message must have a MIME-compatible mail program (or MIME decoder), as well. Not all mail programs support MIME.

NCSA: The National Center for Supercomputing Applications at the University of Illinois at Urbana-Champaign.

Netizen: A term used to describe an Internet user who is aware of the culture and rules governing the Internet.

NETiquette: Derived from the two words Network and Etiquette, these are the rules of participation online. The Internet from the start has been a self-governing society. Knowing what is tolerated and/or allowed by the Internet Community will help you avoid being flamed.

Newbie: A somewhat derogatory term on the Internet meaning an inexperienced and obnoxious new user. The term refers to the brand of user who is unschooled in the Internet's traditions, takes little time to learn them, and acts rudely.

Newsgroups: Another area on the Internet where you can post questions or join discussions. Google groups, located at http://groups.google.com, are where most onliners tap into the Internet newsgroups. Some quick rules to remember:

- When joining a new newsgroup, watch the flow of messages for a few days to discern the group's customs before contributing messages. This is called lurking.

- Do not promote any product you will commercially gain from in any way. Internet users have tried very hard to avoid commercialization since the Internet's inception, and they do not appreciate any deviation from this unwritten rule in discussion groups. Send out an unsolicited e-mail and you could possible receive thousands of flames. Enough to shut down your server or have your ISP cancel your account.

- Keep messages short and on topic.

- Never post the same message to more than one newsgroup, especially if it's a file. There are some users who read many newsgroups daily and don't appreciate reading the same message, or getting the same file, more than once.

- Be sure to review this book and OnlineNetiquette.com in its entirety before you send your first post.

NSF: National Science Foundation, the agency which founded the NSFNET.

NSFnet: One of the "backbone networks" of the Internet.

PPP: An abbreviation for **Point-to-Point Protocol**, a standard for connecting modems, specifically, to the Internet. It is the successor to SLIP.

Phishing: Phishing is a scam that uses spam to deceive consumers into disclosing their personal information. Phishing is considered a two-step scam. First it steals a company's identity and then uses the information to victimize consumers by stealing their credit identities.

Public Domain: While freeware is cost-free, the actual code to public-domain software is available to anyone who wants it. Public-domain software has been refined and modified possibly hundreds of times by people who have the ability to improve it.

Search Engine: A search engine, such Google, is sort of the online version of the yellow pages. By learning each search engine's criteria for searching the Web, you can effectively type in keyword phrases that allow the search engine to pull up a list of all the Web pages that list the information you are looking for. Each search engine operates differently, and each has a section at their site that instructs you on how to use their features for the most accurate outcome.

Server: A central computer from which a particular service takes place. For example, there are FTP servers, Gopher servers, and WAIS servers. Servers are accessed by clients (software).

Shareware: Software for which users must pay a fee after a certain trial period. The trial period is usually thirty days, and the fee is normally lower than the cost of commercial software. Most unregistered shareware is only available in a less-powerful version, with the full version available upon registration. It is strongly recommended that if you like the software and plan on using it pay for it!

SLIP: An abbreviation for Serial Line Interface Protocol. SLIP is a standard for connecting modems, specifically, to the Internet. It has rapidly been succeeded by PPP.

Snail Mail: The online reference to U.S. Postal Mail. Too funny! ;-)

Spam : This term refers to multiple e-mails sent to those who are not interested in what they have to offer. Compare spam to the junk mail you receive in your snail-mail box. It is strongly suggested that you never send unsolicited e-mail to anyone either directly or through their Web site's form. You will get flamed and you may even lose your ISP account as many Internet service providers will disconnect you when they receive complaints about your spamming activities. You can count on other Netizens complaining to your ISP. This practice is not tolerated by the Internet Community as a whole.

Status Bar: This bar at the bottom of your browser's window always indicates the status of your request. It indicates what percentage of the page, file, or graphic being downloaded. Your status bar will reflect "Done" when the downloading is completed.

TCP/IP: The standard for communication among computers connected to the Internet and stands for **Transmission Control Protocol/Internet Protocol**. While it is a relatively slow protocol, it works wonders for intercommunication among different systems.

UNIX: A standard for network operating systems. UNIX has been around for decades and comes in many flavors. For the Internet user, the most common contact with UNIX is the way in which directories are divided. All UNIX directories are separated by forward slashes. For example, "myfiles/mydocuments" might be a directory. Also be aware that UNIX directories are case sensitive; *myfiles* is different, in UNIX, than *MyFiles*. Get in the habit when writing down URLs or e-mail addresses to underline the letters that may be capitalized. In general, most URLs and e-mail addresses will always work when typed in all-small case.

URL: Universal or Uniform Resource Locator. A standard way of representing services on the Internet. A URL usually consists of a scheme name (such as HTTP), followed by a colon, two slashes, and then the address of the site to which you would like to connect.

USENET Newsgroup: A place on the Internet where people can discuss pretty much any topic. Google has fully integrated the past twenty years of Usenet archives into Google groups, which now offers access to more than 845 million messages dating back to 1981.

UUEncode/UUDecode: A method of putting binary files (graphics and/or programs) into an Internet e-mail or newsgroup message.

Printed in the United States
111916LV00004B/302/A